COMPLETING THE ARC

poems by

Nancy A. Hewitt

Finishing Line Press
Georgetown, Kentucky

COMPLETING
THE ARC

Copyright © 2022 by Nancy A. Hewitt
ISBN 978-1-64662-899-5 First Edition
All rights reserved under International and Pan-American Copyright Conventions. No part of this book may be reproduced in any manner whatsoever without written permission from the publisher, except in the case of brief quotations embodied in critical articles and reviews.

ACKNOWLEDGMENTS

My gratitude goes out to the editors of the following journals in which some of the poems in this collection, sometimes in earlier versions, first appeared:

Connecticut River Review: "At the Guggenheim, or Working-Class Girl Meets Rothko"
Halcyone Magazine: "Back in Black," "complications of dusk"
Mid-American Review: "Measured"
Phoebe Journal: "Completing the Arc"

I'm indebted to the many fine faculty members at UMass Boston and the Vermont College of Fine Arts who mentored my work, and to the many peers with whom I've shared poems. And to the women of Kitchen Table Writers, a group which grew from a class at the Joiner Center at UMass Boston one summer in the early 1990s, I'm grateful for nearly 30 years of First Fridays and weekend retreats, and for your unfailing friendship and support.

Publisher: Leah Huete de Maines
Editor: Christen Kincaid
Cover Art: Richard C. Smith
Author Photo: Richard C. Smith
Cover Design: Elizabeth Maines McCleavy

Order online: www.finishinglinepress.com
also available on amazon.com

Author inquiries and mail orders:
Finishing Line Press
PO Box 1626
Georgetown, Kentucky 40324
USA

Table of Contents

Completing the Arc 1

At the Guggenheim, Or Working-Class Girl Meets Rothko 2

Four 3

Duck and Cover 4

Cadeau 5

After Morning Housework 6

Betty Crocker Redux 7

Measured 8

complications of dusk 9

Proximities, Barcelona 10

Miro's Journey 11

At the World Press Photo Exhibit, Centre de Cultura

    Contemporania de Barcelona 12

Willing 14

Light Falling 15

Last Egg in the Box 16

Out of Reverence 17

Borders 18

Here in the Dust 19

All Saints' Eve 20

Burial 21

it comes again to this 22

For Richard

Completing the Arc
> *There's a crack in everything—that's how the light gets in.*
> —Leonard Cohen

A warm front's arriving, blasts of sun knifing their way through thunderous gunmetal clouds. Flames emerge from my hesitant fire, lick the edges of the split wood. Electricity hadn't come to my grandparents' farm when my mother left home in the 1940s to work as a maid. And then tungsten filaments: I like to imagine the first time she flicked a switch in the college professor's house to see light playing over furniture she'd polished to a high sheen. Many years later, I remember the slant of light on the empty green bottle of Rolling Rock as it completed its arc from the open Pontiac window to the shoulder of the rural road lined with autumn's pink poverty grass. In those days before cup-holders and Breathalyzers, before seatbelts, my father would have steadied the bottles between his legs and ordered my mother to heave the empties out of sight. *That never happened*, he said, 30 years later. In the velvety folds of the mind there are desires that lean back in their comfortable chairs, awaiting illumination. Then there's the light offered up by words, and how sometimes we turn away first, before the pain of refusal.

At the Guggenheim, or Working-Class Girl Meets Rothko
Orange and Yellow, 1956

My first time walking up the Guggenheim ramp: two stacked rectangles, orange and yellow-green. I fell into some sort of trance; the Saturday museum crowd vanished. I'd never been alone with orange before. Mine had been a sepia childhood with erratic bursts of fireworks. Sunset was dangerous, a time to look toward ground, fathers due home and mothers flashing red, no attention left to pay to the incidental sky. Since then, I've been schooled in calmer sunsets—the fine art of looking out and up, the distant peaceful co-existence of reds, purples, greens and blues. But I was not prepared for Rothko that day, how rectangles of color could lift off the canvas, hang there so stridently, for no practical reason—two wide swaths, radiating waves, not meant to compete. Shimmering in my mind decades later: two colors bleeding into each other—neither taking over, neither giving in. Separate but not alone.

Four

You were four, on the floor with your coloring book,
says Aunt Bev, 89, remembering a family visit
65 years ago—*and you began crying: One of your crayons
was broken. I'm not saying you broke it*, she says
quickly, recalling my distress at making mistakes,
just that somehow it got broken. It was a summer day,
1950, in her large, bright living room with faded
green ceiling-to-floor drapes, a worn wood floor.
I would have been intent on coloring within
the lines. They'd have all been smoking—
my father and his brother, my mother and Bev—
but it's only my aunt I picture, smiling then
as now, pulling on her Lucky Strike,
gray eyes squinting in the exhale, while
in some other space hovered my father's
other children, the unspeakable divorce.
Today she continues, *I got down on the floor
and tried to tape your crayon.* The waxy feel
and smell of Crayola—Venetian red, burnt
umber—each wrapper just slightly more muted
than the crayon itself. At four, I thought
that if a crayon broke I would never have
that color again. Today she tells me that all
but one of my four half-siblings have died.
She knows the last one and he knows of me.
Back then I didn't know that crayons
could be mended, that after the mistake,
when you peeled back the paper,
you would still have color.

Duck and Cover
Civil Defense Film, 1951

We didn't know why Russia wanted to hurt us, but the man's serious, stern voice seemed to speak to each of us, assuring us he had a plan to keep us safe. In the movie, kids who looked just like us ducked under their desks and laced their fingers together behind their heads to save them from the heat of the bomb. Kids walking to school and on their bikes, and even a farm boy driving a tractor, all dropped to the ground, then found a wall or a curb to curl up against. And not until the kindly air warden touched you on the shoulder was it safe to get up. The serious voice said that if the bomb hit when we were at home, we could count on our parents to have a safety plan. Most families, he assured us, had built a bomb shelter or at least had stocks of canned goods in the basement. And it was important to stay far away from windows. I wanted to believe him, but he didn't tell us trailer kids where we should go. When salesmen came to the door, my mother and I hid, kneeling on the bedroom floor. To stay safe during Hurricane Hazel, we stayed in the car overnight. But now from the man with the stern voice, I began to fear broken glass. In my family, safety had always meant my father coming home right after work. Nights he was late, dinner turned black in the oven while my mother watched by the window, fearful he would stagger in the door, slur his words, then turn angry when we didn't laugh at his jokes. I shared her worries without saying so, held them safe inside me, a package tied up with string. Did she also worry about where we'd hide if the bomb dropped? In a cloud of cigarette smoke, she waited for the threat of tires coming up the drive. There were so many windows in the trailer, and under it, only air.

Cadeau

after Man Ray: Cadeau, *1921, Cast iron with brown patina*

Spring, 1943: My mother stands behind her new husband on the running board of his new Ford. They grin for the camera, she in a dark dress with a white ruffled collar, he in a dark suit. Black and white, before color. Her arm circles his neck, his hand on her wrist, but whether to caress or to loosen her grip is a matter of conjecture. He was 30 and had rescued her from the farm, a life lit by kerosene lamps, with no running water and floors that could never be swept clean. Unlike his first wife, with her wandering eye, this 19-year-old girl was well trained in keeping house, would be happy to get up at 5 to cook the eggs, bacon and home fries he expected before heading to the construction site, pack his lunch bucket and have a hot dinner waiting. And in exchange, no more maids' uniforms for her.

And in the beginning, it was so. She was thrilled to manage her own home, especially loved the clean smell of steam when she ironed, as she smoothed out wrinkles, pressed his work shirts, the sheets, even his underwear. But before too long, she grew discontent, from loneliness, his drinking. And as the years moved on, when neighbors would drive her to bars to find him—well, he didn't think he'd married the kind of girl who'd make a scene.

The effects of the nails showed up slowly. First he noticed pulled threads here and there in his jockeys. He put this down to slivers from the wooden clothespins she used to pin laundry to the line. When holes began to appear in his shirts, she claimed ignorance. He tried to ignore the pinpricks of doubt in his mind. It would be much later that he found the source, a flat-iron she'd stashed in the back of a closet, a row of fourteen rusty nails right down the center. He tried to make sense of it: He'd thought she loved electricity.

After Morning Housework
    after Fabritius: The Goldfinch, *1654*

How sweet, that year of coffee klatch afternoons, early 1950s,
the air fragrant with coffee, maybe a cake in the oven, in the
housewives' trailer park kitchens. Older kids in school, I had all

the mothers to myself. Morning chores, written in stone—
Monday laundry, Tuesday ironing. Then the women were free
to gossip, share recipes, review new brands of cake mixes,

complain about husbands. In the era when many men forbade
their wives from working, those afternoons were islands of safety.
While I kept precisely within the lines in my coloring books, I

often heard: *Mine doesn't know the difference from homemade.* Then
peals of laughter, how "the girls" finished each other's sentences,
all of them in this together. I got an earful of *Guiding Light*

gossip—*Why doesn't she leave him? … should just hide the liquor*—
and before long, the women's actual lives entered the room: *then
he wants to be all lovey dovey … a brassy blonde, saw her with*

my own eyes. I took it all in, the hard work of being a wife—
loose women on the prowl, how men just couldn't help
themselves. Stage-whispered secrets and tears: Marriage, or

something about it, seemed to be at fault. Decades later, I find
myself drawn to a book about a painting stolen from a museum.
On the cover, an image of *The Goldfinch.* A gilt, ornamental cage

holds a delicately painted bird, feathers and bone in muted grays
and yellows and its leg, no thicker than a twig, chained to its
perch. I consider: Why doubly bound? Ah, to prevent

the singing. One tiny dot of light in its eye, a glint on the chain.

Betty Crocker Redux

Tissue paper bridges rose above us in dreams,
while below we engaged in the manual
labors of our days, our pencils and books,
our pots and pans. Inhaled throat-
constricting road dust, coughed
to no avail. Toxic days, unless
you were masked. The mask of meals.
Behind the times, my mother stayed
Betty Crocker, toiled nightly at her stove.
As night drew near, the driveway stones
would commence to rattle. A smolder
of macaroni and cheese, or spaghetti
growing thick as worms. Hours by the window
in a Lucky Strikes fog. On occasion my father
would offer up venison or frogs' legs,
to be eaten on slurred command.
Eggs of the snapping turtle were a delicacy,
though gritty. The three of us popped up
and down like jack-in-the-boxes—to serve,
to demand, to leave—all out of turn,
all hide-and-you-will-be-sought,
our everyday Halloween masks.

Measured

Home Economics, circa 1963: My search for precision was sated. Sift flour into the measuring cup, level it with a knife blade, then alternate dry and wet ingredients, always beginning and ending with dry. Measure before cutting fabrics, and always obey the folds. Follow the carpenters' rule of thumb: *Measure twice, cut once.* In 1970, my father took the measure of my new mini-skirt and declared it lacking, refused to allow me in his car. I found it difficult to measure up, as did the rest of his family, his workers, his wives. Even the doctors who made house calls disappointed, just wanted his money. Weeks every winter with infected tonsils, I counted the hours inhaling camphorated oil-laden air, waiting for the doctor, waiting for the silver column of mercury to climb up the glass cylinder, to tell the numbers—my temperature, the too-expensive bill. Every year now the health department exhorts me to trade in my mercury for digitals, but I would miss the shake-down, its slow crawl. After all, in ancient China mercury was believed to prolong life, was given orally to heal fractures. Trouble has so many measures. Atmospheric conditions are measured by degrees of clarity. The Twin Towers fell on a day pilots described as *severe clear*—crisp, sunny, infinite blue skies. On another severe clear Tuesday 10 years later, U.S. Marines killed Osama bin Laden. For proof, they took photographs, retrieved bone marrow samples, swabbed for DNA, and at the last minute decided on one more instrument, based on bin Laden's presumed height of 6 feet 4. The body bag was zipped open, and with no tape measure available, a 6-foot Marine lay down beside the corpse, which, as they eyeballed it, was four inches longer than the Marine, a final imprecise dimension before the body was tossed into the sea. On the Ground Zero memorial, the algorithm for listing the dead is by *meaningful adjacencies*: friends who worked in adjacent cubicles, people who jumped to their deaths holding hands.

complications of dusk
        in memory of J.D.

no freedom for a ten-year-old
like a June-dusk Friday
sliding by slow degrees into night
your friends your bikes your good citizen award
how two months ago you pulled a man to shore
just doing what I should picture in the paper
now night is busy shadowing your bike
on the other side of the tracks did you say
did your brother say *Mom will kill me / you if*
to track the words that might have hung
in the air that mild night when you ran to get it
you good child did you look both ways
the 8:04 the 8:05 crossing paths right on time
were the street lights glowing there's a way
dusk complicates the senses may I erase
your run into grays and irons walk us back
to cheat your pace perhaps trace back
to a blacksmith hear the bang see the melt
of molten steel born of good intention vibration
of forged steel may I blame night
when fused with rails dissolved your bike
into neutrals how we try to see under over it
did you feel a twitch hear the ring
of rails black steel hardened to something
that can be traced will we remember
that the rails like a spring night like you
always meant to deliver good

Proximities, Barcelona

the unscreened windows of Barcelona
tonight at Can Treso our table against
a wall and just outside the open window
a young couple on stools the man's bulky
thigh in black denim a foot away
his black leather bag strapped over
his shoulder nudging the wall
to fend off pickpockets I slice the muscle
of Iberian pork served on a slab
of black slate two wine glasses inside
two beer bottles outside a beggar
approaches the couple a clink of coins
by the time we reach our hotel a scream
of swifts is circling the garden
neither naming nor indicting

Miro's Journey
from the Miro Foundation, Barcelona

In the beginning, the country house, grape vines,
reassuring brush strokes, green and orange.
Then *eclectic*—a wild beast of Fauvism,
vermilion and ultramarine, facets
of Cubism. Catalan freedom fighter
and creator of a private universe,
the Constellations, painted in Normandy
during blackouts. Canvasses of birds,
women and stars rolled under his arm,
he fled Paris for Mallorca, 1939.
After the student riots, Paris, '68,
burned forests appeared—"Flame
in Space and Nude Woman." Last gasps
of Franco brought on the *savage paintings.*
Painting disgusts me profoundly, he said.
He carved with a knife, tortured
and burned his canvasses. Roiled
cobalt paint, from 1973, right in front
of me, still bubbled up, so close I can
smell the char, the burnt stretchers.
I've crossed over the distance
that visitors are required to keep.
I lean in close enough to see
brushstrokes, yet I'm not noticed
by the three young guards
across the room who yawn, chat,
tap their cell phones to search
for messages, answers.
Las Ramblas yet to be savaged.

At the World Press Photo Exhibit, Centre de Cultura Contemporania de Barcelona
June, 2017

a Russian woman just awakened in Luhansk her bombed house her belted black robe handkerchief to her eyes green apples blasted off the tree fallen as if from strong wind dusty 78 RPMs in the foreground warped by heat men in Aleppo step over rubble pass babies along the line a mass grave in Mosul so

many feet bound together bones exposed a line of Chinese children against a wall at a sports school undergo the required 30 minutes a day of toe-pressure training a man hangs from a crane in Iran after public flogging the weight-lifter from Halifax with no hands smiles into the camera as do beaming runners

caught in mid-sprint forensics show an endangered black rhino in Aleppo tried to run fell to his knees shot at close range the bloodied head the missing tusk loggerhead turtles trailing skeins of fishing net still swim still swim blood seeps through a baby's bandages drips on concrete spatters on fallen

businessmen on mothers on strangers to each other blood on walls blood still wet Philippine drug war stacks 3000 inmates on stairs to sleep head to foot men in panda suits search for radio signals cradle retrieved panda cubs the lengths to which we may go to hold what needs us Castro's waxy glare from his

coffin but I'm transfixed by a mating panda pair the male's mouth open in grinning ecstasy the female stolid as a table bearing his weight the species at stake a moose head defrosts on a Russian table the lips a delicacy a house where white dogs cross-bred with wolves sleep outside all winter hold the vigil

stare at us from porches couch springs escaping sunflowers grow out of cracks on a deserted Ukrainian road a man rakes the soil his back to earth mounds to abandoned houses the plants respond by living a girl in Mosul backs up against her house her daily life oil fields belching smoke tanks roiling dust her eyes say *I'll do anything just make this stop* another girl doesn't dream now *I'm not afraid of anything anymore* her mother's hand rests on her forehead as if to close her hazel eyes her eyes refuse

Willing

Last night's flight home: Rays of the setting sun smudge
    the clouds into a crazy-quilt of color,

and the surge of possibility rises up in me as if
    to boil over—late December, the time of day

that prompts shore birds to scurry, purples the proud hills.
    Somewhere in Ukraine, an old man, dressed

in his best suit, grateful to wait in line for hours to cast
    his very first vote. A man in Sierra Leone

prints his toes for identification after his hands are cut off.
    The woman in the zocalo in Mexico City born

without arms crochets the finest lace with her toes,
    nails painted turquoise. How often we look away.

The pharmacist continues to fill his amber bottles,
    the shoemaker to secure his rivets, while

a father stares into his whiskey glass and a mother's gaze
    lingers on every headlight, willing

each car to come up the drive, her vigil lasting long
    after the orange horizon has vanished.

Light Falling
Howard Hodgkin, 2015

Wide lush strokes of deep umber
like planks of wood closing in on you. Light can feel
heavy sometimes, falling instead of fading. Dark rectangles
extend to the ceiling if you let them, hemming you
further into the last year of your life. Do you feel it
coming? Do you paint yourself in to or out of the box?
This slanted scene: Maybe you're on an ocean liner
buffeted by waves, the sea roiling in layers of green, raw umber,
the small window of your cabin capturing sunset, crimped
brushwork on the left like a memory, an invitation to live in that
rectangle of light and just dream, dream about a cargo carrier
approaching from the right, the thready cadmium lines, a mystery
vessel of gossamer intention, tangerine sunset glowing
through its transparency, posing a veiled question
for the Naples yellow on the wall, a hinge of color
opened up like a shutter. Maybe you detected
motion, the swish of dying light. A simple slant
and pitch, reflection into a dark wood room,
the brush pressed firm and broad, day
by day until it owned you.

Last Egg in the Box
    after an untitled photograph by Kari Gunter-Seymour

Something eludes the camera here,
something behind darkness, behind night.
Life, in abeyance, within that rough shell.
Or life abandoned, left behind
in a corrugated box in a darkened room.
One left. If this were the last egg on earth,
what would you want it to birth?
A dinosaur? A crow? An Einstein?
The egg is nestled between spacers,
rows that could be temples rising
from dark earth, the sides too uneven
to be scaled. In the Mayan ballgame,
a twenty-pound rubber ball was moved
around a court by teams of players using
their trunks, hips and upper arms
to keep it in the air, hands and feet
forbidden. The game was a portal
to the underworld, human sacrifice
often the result. Some depictions
show the ball to be the severed head
of the loser. Centuries later, a version
of this game is still played. Imagine a sliver
of dark moon that blots out roughness,
the way it curls around potential.

Out of Reverence

El Charco: a nature preserve in San Miguel, a furrowed
network of dusty pathways—we pass in and out
of blazing sun that February day following our guide,

an American expat, through the shadows of hulking cacti.
Many rare or endangered species find sanctuary here,
some rescued from building sites cleared in the wake

of the spreading city. We edge our way along narrow trails
carved around skeletons of long-dead trees, now homes
for insects, opportunities for birds. He cautions us

on the tripping hazards of tangled roots, the condition
known locally as *fallen gringo syndrome*. A hummingbird
flits by: *Thought to be reincarnated warriors*, says our guide,

then points to resurrection ferns on the north side
of the trail, able to remain dormant for 100 years. Ahead
and to our left, an enormous canyon comes into view.

It holds the deep green pool which names this refuge:
El Charco del Ingenio. *How deep is the pool?* I ask.
I like measurements, like to know the elements that define

a culture. I like knowing that a local indigenous people
speaks Purepecho, one of 62 distinct languages spoken
in Mexico. And that only in 2003 did the government

give all indigenous peoples the right to speak
their own tongue. Our guide pauses to gaze at the pool:
Out of reverence, it has never been measured.

Borders
    San Miguel de Allende, 2019

Satie, smooth, in La Mesa Grande. Hollowed-out eyes
of a skeleton stare from a textured stone wall. Yesterday,
a bull's head in a swirl on a bathroom tile, today gone.
Spikes ring the tops of courtyard columns to keep pigeons
from nesting—no second-guessing. Poinsettias grow into
trees to form boundaries. Yet even here, far from where
the Rio Grande used to be, my mother reaches me. She's
a wave that laps over me, laps over me, from the grave.
Even a knife-edge line like mine cannot defeat the swim
of her. Birds wing their way across the wall just north
of here. Mice compress their own flesh to earn passage.
Wind-blown seeds, insects insinuate themselves through
chinks. Wafting scent of jalapenos, the sulfur of gunpowder,
dust of centuries. Coyotes watch for prey. The weather
of will.

Here in the Dust
   for my mother

    Here on a bench in a dusty wind in a San Miguel courtyard, I think of you. *Why go to Mexico again?* you'd chide. Here is where I tell you: to feel these warm stones under my feet, to be surrounded by color, to see workers with pickaxes who to this day carry stone slabs on their backs.

    I go back to the work of the dusty farmyard: Grandma boils water in a copper vat, while Grandpa beheads chickens for Sunday dinner. How the grown-ups laugh when I turn my head from the chickens' careening bodies, when Grandpa pulls me to his scratchy face, too close to his whiskey breath.

    Beheading, a word you didn't know, the price paid for journalists speaking the truth. You wouldn't have survived knowing of these murders, nor would you have survived Kayla's suicide by rifle. And now that I am no longer your buffer against pain, I am free to feel my own.

    Dust, stone, wind—back to beginnings. Fear lives everywhere. Trouble sidles in more closely. You and I have known trouble, have known drought. A friend says, *We live the lives that our parents couldn't.* What do you think about that? What I mean is, now that I use language to open the skies.

All Saints' Eve

Maybe it was our bonfire of tree roots, still
sending up steady plumes of smoke
that made its way into my dream,
where a family of foxes
emerged from under the bed
into a fog that held us all, the kits
nipping each other in play,
the adults sniffing the air
with their long, pointed snouts,
then all of us evaporating into deeper fog.

I awake to a morning fog that envelops me,
then dissipates in a flash, opens up
a clear view of the near field. Frost caps
on a few lamb's-ears at the bottom
of the steps, and on the terrace
a shimmer of scarlet and fuchsia,
geraniums in wan sun.
I remember the foxes' burnished
red coats, long black legs,
the tangled troupe of kits,
how facile their disappearance…
Is it better to remember or to forget?

Last week an elderly neighbor, out of wood,
determined to keep his stove ablaze,
began to burn his library of books
in no particular order, some signed,
some overrun with marginalia.
Staying alive is no easy matter.
I'm reminded of squatters
in British short stories who burn
their furniture,
stick by stick,
then start in on the molding.

Burial

When we bury our fourth cat, my husband says
it's the last time he can do this, heave
the shovel down through Vermont clay
thick with root tangle, solid with ledge,
dig a four-foot hole for the fourth
wood coffin he's built by hand.
Our silent agreement: that their bodies
will remain intact—the orange and white,
the calico, the gray tabby and now
Sebastian, Maine coon
with long black fur, a tuxedo chest.

We have a dog now, and a fifth cat.
My husband mows wide paths that disappear
into the woods' darkness,
sows grass seed along the old farm lane.
We add a stone terrace, a shed and cold frame.
I learn from a nursery clerk
that the difference between an eight-
and a ten-foot sapling is six years,
and we choose the larger ones,
plant five maple saplings to form
an alee along the driveway.
As if we'll never die.
Or live on through them.

In the wet part of the field we plant
a young weeping willow, its limbs upright,
still reaching for height.
I'd assumed these trees lived
their whole lives with graceful,
flowing limbs. Now I wonder out loud
how long it takes
for a willow to begin to weep.

it comes again to this

here I am lost again another mis-
labeled intersection merging
with my misguided sense
of direction when you appear
this time wearing white
your dark gaze a museum portrait
my guide as I search
for the salt-veined river
remember the ways
you have saved me
wresting the truth
from mourners at the grave
how you know
that when darkness arrives
these roads still connect
and how knowing
does not mean dis-
solving so in this way I find
the porch by the river
see a split rock on the other shore
and you leave me
to consider how
this lightning strike occurred
unobserved a purple orchid
leaning against the screen

Raised in the mid-Atlantic states, **Nancy Hewitt** worked in research laboratories in Pennsylvania and in Boston before deciding to enter the field of social work. She earned her MSW from the Simmons College School of Social Work, then worked in community mental health settings in the Boston area before establishing a psychotherapy practice in Salem, MA, where she worked for over 30 years.

Her interests in poetry and personal writing were paths to offering journal therapy workshops in her practice, and she published both poetry and fiction in *The Use of Personal Narratives in the Helping Professions: A Teaching Casebook*.

Throughout her social work career, she studied poetry, receiving a Certificate in Creative Writing from UMass Boston, followed by a residency at the Vermont Studio Center, then by earning an MFA in poetry from the Vermont College of Fine Arts. Her work has been published in *Mid-American Review, Connecticut River Review, The Ekphrastic Review, Ellipsis, Halcyone Magazine* and other journals. Her poems have been awarded the Editor's Prize from both *Jabberwock Review* and *Spoon River Poetry Review*. Her chapbook *Heard* was published by Finishing Line Press in 2013.

She feels most inspired by the natural world, from the hills and fields of Vermont to the colorful streetscapes of San Miguel de Allende, Barcelona and Lisbon. Her love of story is seen in her narrative style, and she feels an affinity toward ekphrastic work. The smallest details of a story or a scene engage her, and her hope is that readers will identify with these moments that inform her poems.

Hewitt was the first Poet Laureate of Swampscott, MA. She and her husband, architect Richard Smith, divide their time between Massachusetts and East Randolph, VT.

www.ingramcontent.com/pod-product-compliance
Lightning Source LLC
LaVergne TN
LVHW041521070426
835507LV00012B/1738